A Gratitude Book
for Children

Goodness Gracious

Kathleen A. Green

Illustrated by Lori McElrath Eslick

Dear Reader,

Have you ever felt so happy that it seemed like your whole body was smiling and you wanted to say thank you out loud? Have you ever been so glad for something in your life, like a friend or your favorite food or the way the grass smells, that you wanted to do a happy dance? Or maybe a thank you dance?! Saying thank you for all the awesome things—big and little—is what some people do when they pray, and what some people do when they meditate, and what some people do when they just sit and think.

Maybe you don't know who or what you're thanking but that's perfectly ok. It still feels good to remind yourself just how good some things are and how much you love them. If you practice saying thank you each day for the things you feel good about, you might find yourself feeling happier and more peaceful every day. I have friends who call their thank you before eating or going to sleep a blessing or grace. I just call it a thankful thought. And whenever I'm not feeling very happy and need to remember all the awesome things about life, or when I feel so full of thank yous that it seems my heart might burst, I take time for a thankful thought!

You can say thank you with someone else or all by yourself. You can say it when you are walking or playing, or sitting at the dinner table, or lying in bed before you go to sleep. You can sing it, dance it, draw it, or just think about it quietly inside your head. You can have a thankful thought anywhere and any time. The most important thing is feeling thankful and showing it! This book is made up of lots of thankful thoughts that can help you practice saying thank you.

One thing I say thank you for is that you're out there reading this book, and I hope, starting to think about making up some thankful thoughts of your very own.

With love and a great big thank you,

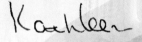

Everything begins from a tiny little seed.
Apple trees and grains for bread and
other foods we need.
The seed is planted. A tiny beginning.
And with lots of love and care,
the tiny seed grows, just like me.
Tiny beginnings are everywhere!

We are thankful for the food,
for the sun, and the moon.
We give thanks for everything
that is good.

Can be sung to the tune of London Bridge

Time to eat and time to say
thank you for this meal today.
For the hands that plant the wheat,
for the foods I love to eat,
I will take the time to say
thank you, thank you every day.

Can be sung to the tune of ABCs

We give thanks for mac and cheese,
broccoli, apples too.
And we thank the people who
grow and pick our food.

We give thanks for orange juice,
scrambled eggs, pancakes too.
And we thank the people who
make our yummy food.

Add in your own favorite foods
and make up your own verses!
Can be sung to the tune of
Mary Had A Little Lamb.

I say a little prayer with my body calm and still.
I say a little prayer and close my eyes, I will.
I say a little prayer with my head gently bowed.
I say a little prayer and my voice is not too loud.
I say a little prayer with my heart open wide.
I hope that all people, everywhere, find peace and love inside.

Thank you sky so bright and blue.
Thank you sun for all you do;
for shining on the dragonfly, and frog and
inchworm passing by.
Thank you birds who sing so sweet.
Thank you grass beneath my feet;
so green, so cool, so soft to touch.
I love to dance and roll in such.
For all the goodness that you bring,
I thank you earth for everything.

My friends come in all shapes and sizes.
No two are exactly alike.
My friends and I like to share with each other.
Sometimes even our bikes!
My friends are the best when they
giggle with me.
And when my friends cry or feel bad
they should know
I love my friends,
Because they're special, my friends,
and I wish them blessings wherever they go.

Thank you furry friends who love to meow and bark;
playing fetch and hide-and-seek at home or in the park.
Thank you feathered friends who fly up in the sky;
nesting in the swaying trees and soaring right on by.
Thank you slithering friends who relax in the noontime sun;
stretching out or curling up. It looks like so much fun!
Thank you swimming friends who live in oceans, tanks and seas;
gliding through water with fins and gills, saying "Come swim along,
if you please."
I'm thankful for all of my animal friends:
the short and the small, the big and the tall.
Yes, I'm thankful for them all.

I am thankful for my teachers who teach me things I need to know.
I am thankful for my teachers who care about me as I grow.
I am thankful for my teachers who ask me why I'm mad.
I am thankful for my teachers who help me when I'm sad.
I am thankful for my teachers who show me how to love and share.
I am thankful for my teachers. That's why I say this little prayer.

Thank teachers by name.

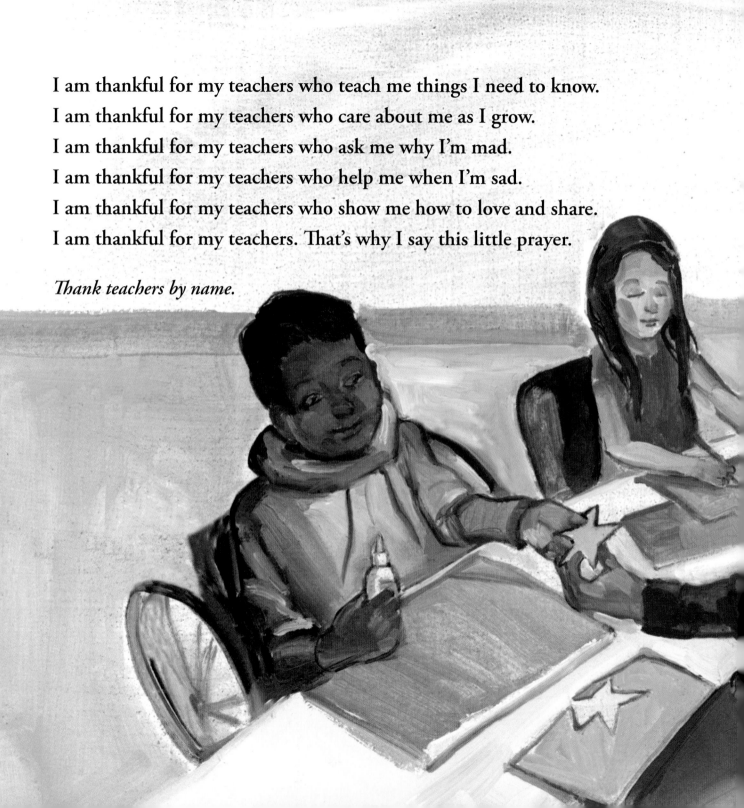

Some families have brothers, some families have sisters,
some families have both. Some have none.
Some families have grandparents and aunties and pets.
Whether big or small awesome families have fun.
Some families have one mommy and some families have two.
It's the same way with daddies you see.
Just think of all the awesome families made of love;
loving you, loving me.

My eyes see beauty all around.

My ears hear music—a lovely sound.

My nose smells fresh air and a pretty red flower.

My tongue can taste salty, sweet, and sour.

My hands touch gently and with loving care.

My heart is filled with thanks to share.

I don't know why some things go away.
Like when the cat and the goldfish died.
Or when my grandma moved far, far away.
My heart was hurt and I cried.
I don't understand and sometimes I worry
that other things will go away too.
Like when Mommy gets sick or my brother goes
to school.
I worry and then I feel blue.
So I take a deep breath and I share how I feel
with someone who loves me and cares.
It helps me calm down, turns my frown upside down.
I am thankful that someone was there.

My body is amazing! Have you seen what I can do?

My body is amazing! Just look and I'll show you.

I have feet that jump and run.

I have hands that clap and play.

I have a heart that beats with love.

And I have a mind that learns each day.

Just look at all the amazing things that I can do.

Like dancing, singing, laughing, thinking, and saying "I love you"!

Move around and say other great things your body can do!

I am full of wonder. I ask What? Why? And How?

I like to question and discover new things.

Sometimes I just have to say "Wow"!

Cause the world is full of wonder too:

Fluffy clouds in the sky. Giant whales in the sea.

Wonder-full world. Wonder-full me.

Yes, I am full of wonder. I ask What? Why? How? And more!

Cause the world is so very wonderful and I love to explore!

Planet earth is beautiful!
It's the place that I call home.
I love her deserts, lakes, and beaches,
and all the places that animals roam.
I'm amazed at her forests and mountains,
so wide and oh so grand!
I will help keep Earth clean and safe
for all the creatures who live on this land.
Planet earth is beautiful!
It's the home I love and share.
So I will treat it gently, with lots of loving care.

Sparkling just like twinkle lights in the dark night sky,
the stars are oh so beautiful. O-o-o-h and ah-h-h, I sigh!
Glowing like a big nightlight, what an awesome thing.
The moon is oh so beautiful. O-o-o-h and ah-h-h, I sing!
Like a smile so wide and bright, a brilliant beaming ball.
The sun is oh so beautiful. O-o-o-h and ah-h-h, that's all!

Can be sung to the tune of Row Your Boat.

My mind thinks of ways to be thoughtful.
My mouth chooses words that are true.
My hands try to always be helpful.
Every day I say "thank you."

With my heart open wide,
I am grateful.
With my family by my side,
I am grateful.
With helping hands so bold,
I am grateful.
With kindness to be told,
I am grateful.
With all the joy that I can hold I say,
I am grateful.

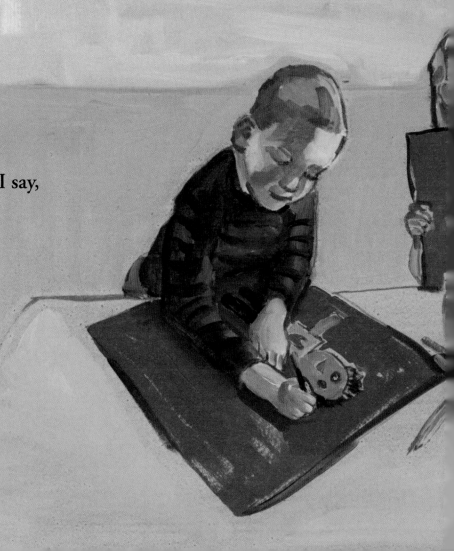

They tell me no monsters live under my bed.

But sometimes I'm still a bit scared.

They tell me no monsters hide out in my room.

But look for myself? I don't dare!

They tell me it's just my imagination. That's all.

But my imagination says monsters are real.

They tell me they'll check again, make sure I'm safe.

They say, "We understand how you feel."

Then they tell me they love me and give me a hug.

And that's when it's finally clear.

As I drift off to sleep, tucked in tight, safe and sound,

I know there are no monsters. Not here.

As I go to sleep tonight,

Please, love, hug my family tight.

With stars and moon so big and bright

Love shines round me like a light.

As I go to sleep tonight,

Please, love, hug my family tight.

Can be sung to the tune of Twinkle, Twinkle Little Star.

It's quiet time. It's time for sleep.

Body rests. Heart softly beats.

Before I dream or start to snore I think of all I'm thankful for…

(*Name aloud friends, family, and anything else you're feeling
especially thankful for.*)

I've said my thanks with love so deep.

Now it's time to go to sleep.

Sometimes I feel sad, and sometimes I cry.

Sometimes I feel angry, and sometimes I don't know why.

Sometimes I feel confused, or scared, or happy.

Sometimes I feel like yelling, and sometimes I feel snappy.

Sometimes I feel hopeful and wish upon a star.

Sometimes I feel quiet and calm; thinking about the way things are.

I have lot of feelings and I feel lots of ways

like excited, or even silly.

I feel _____ today.

I'm glad that I have feelings because they're an important part of me.

I'm glad I can share my feelings because my name is _____

and it's the only me that I can be!

To my captain, Mitchell,
who guided the ship for 30 years but sailed off
into the great unknown just before this
work of love was published.
Couldn't have done it without him! —KG

Copyright © 2019 by Kathleen A. Green. All rights reserved. Published by
Skinner House Books, an imprint of the Unitarian Universalist Association,
a liberal religious organization with more than 1,000 congregations in the U.S.
and Canada, 24 Farnsworth St., Boston, MA 02210–1409.

www.skinnerhouse.org

Printed in the United States

print ISBN: 978-1-55896-832-5
eBook ISBN: 978-1-55896-845-5

6 5 4 3 2 1 / 23 22 21 20 19

CIP data is on file with the Library of Congress